NATIONAL GEOGRAPHIC

D0100740

Kitchen Rules

Wil Spencer

Contents

Kitchen Rules 3

Before You Start 4

When You Are Cooking 6

After You Have Finished 9

Kitchen Rules

Cooking in the kitchen can be fun. But cooking can also be dangerous. Rules can help make the kitchen a safer place.

Before You Start

Your hair may be carrying germs. A hair tie or hat will keep your hair away from the food.

Your hands may also carry germs. Clean hands will keep the food free from germs.

When You Are Cooking

Knives are very sharp. Adults know how to handle knives safely.

Hot things can cause burns. Adults know how to use the stove or oven without getting hurt.

Spills can make the floor slippery. Wiping up spills right away will keep people from slipping.

After You Have Finished

Turn off the stove or oven.

If the stove or oven is left on,
it could start a fire.
Always turn the stove or oven off.

When you are finished cooking, wipe the benches and sweep the floor. This will keep the kitchen clean.

Follow these rules when you cook. They will help make the kitchen a safer place.